SAINT CONSEQUENCE

SAINT

CONSEQUENCE

POEMS

MICHAEL M.

WEINSTEIN

ALICE JAMES BOOKS

NEW GLOUCESTER, MAINE · ALICEJAMESBOOKS.ORG

10 9 8 7 6 5 4 3 2 1

Alice James Books are published by Alice James Poetry Cooperative, Inc.

Alice James Books
Auburn Hall
60 Pineland Drive, Suite 206
New Gloucester, ME 04260
www.alicejamesbooks.org

Library of Congress Cataloging-in-Publication Data

Names: Weinstein, Michael M., 1987- author
Title: Saint consequence / Michael M. Weinstein.
Other titles: Saint consequence (Compilation)
Description: New Gloucester, Maine : Alice James Books, 2025.
Identifiers: LCCN 2025001617 (print) | LCCN 2025001618 (ebook) | ISBN
9781949944747 trade paperback | ISBN 9781949944464 epub
Subjects: LCGFT: Poetry
Classification: LCC PS3623.E4324474 S25 2025 (print) | LCC PS3623.E4324474
(ebook) | DDC 811/.6--dc23/eng/20250307
LC record available at https://lccn.loc.gov/2025001617
LC ebook record available at https://lccn.loc.gov/2025001618]

Alice James Books gratefully acknowledges support from individual donors, private foundations, the National Endowment for the
Arts, and the Poetry Foundation (https://www.poetryfoundation.org).

Cover photo: Megan Bent, C-Spine Lordosis, 2018, chlorophyll print on coprosma leaf

Table of Contents

ADDENDUM TO THE BOOK OF MARVELS AND TRAVELS

And then I changed.

The hilltop burst with phlox and daffodils   impossible
to scale.   The city block was all torn up

but kept   and sat getting raggedy-edged in a drawer of September
like lovers' letters —

once windows   now mirrors   thanks
                                        to a loss of address.

The old hopes obsolesced   but purposes
clung like a smell   a past effort etched into
the butter churn   into the telephone's plastic.   When

the fall sun struck them   they *belonged*
as my aqua polka dot dress

with starched white cuffs belonged on a different body
one with less anger
                        less history.   Yet the same

looking isn't just lateness — it's
soft as moldgristle on raspberries   thick as a promise
misheard   cherished   as an artificial

valve allowing doubts a means of egress from the heart

held close for all these years and now

                        yanked out

with the bloodshine wet on it.   It's those ache-
dark gaps we kept   between our smiles and   each tooth

that cavity lie at the root of the truth
this shaft of sunlight warm across the phantom

limb of my name

THEN

"A picture held us captive. And we could not get outside it, for it lay in our language and language seemed to repeat it to us inexorably."

—Ludwig Wittgenstein,
Philosophical Investigations § 115

CUT

The first time, don't remember.
The second, your blue eye
split across the edge of cut-

glass coffee table, saw blurred white
carpet blooms flare wide. That kid,
the one spreadeagled on the mulch,

scooped up pits-first by some-other-
tot-on-the-swingset's mother, who
wept, the scraped knee, the whole bit —

was you, duh. Next time, paired up with
Angela, the blind girl, as she gripped
your wrist in fingerbones, wrenching it

over and over the finish line
of the three-legged race, your chin
split, coursed. Fast blood made a carnation

burst on blouse. The nurse
was one Miss Prinn. She stuffed a dollar
into your red hand and hissed, *Stop crying*.

Then mostly for years no one touched this.

A needle, a dog, a fist, a man in France
— touched is not the right word — *rearranged* you
under your life's last skirt, tossed

you off staircase — cobbles, scraped knee,
the whole bit. Torn culotte.
Then none, until hairy hands

of the doctor cupped the left breast, speculator
over holdings, musing all
dispassionate, *Can we*

claim this as a medical necessity? The blue
Sharpie marker slashed an X
across each nipple — it would cost

extra to replace them. Crookedly
scar grins stitched under the stretched erasure
yank each which way. Burn. Harden and sink

into earth of flesh. One last cut left
no mark — yet the milky negative testified
invaders had entered. Vibrations, the rattle

of infinitesimal hammers driving nails deep
in. Now worn-down bone doors swivel open,
each cleft gasps — as shards of air

wedge in crevices between the tense
of each act, weave your gait into the lapse
of the horse who gallops, gallops, jumps

the fence — no, you can't thread it back through the flesh,
the thrill of impact as both feet hit

earth. Cut. Watch the past unspool

behind you in curls from its canister — you were *her*,
a double, two daughter cells borne from the rip
in the film of one woman and one man, spliced together.

GENDER CLINIC

for Jules Gill-Peterson

The world is made out of forms after all
stopped from becoming   for years
there were questions and then
there were questions would've
stomped the heads off all the dandelions
in the silent film of named emotions
if you'd let them   as a gorgeous

ghost comes close each time you turn
away   sun in your faces
juddering of diesel engines   benedictions
upon the expansion of empire
into our bodies where it has always
been   I believe we were children
small shriek haunting our laughter

and some grown up cut up the chicken
fingers and splurged out the ketchup
and what was time anyway   nobody else
like us existed and we were everywhere
radiant and destructive like weather
the rip in the packet   what came out
whether or not it belonged there

calmly state your terror
then the hold music   hold music
searching the cracks for a pattern   that's
where it began in the dirt in the ammonite

dirt in the drawer full of meanwhile
kept closed so long   I said *boy* I said *ball*
what else do you want me to say

NEAR-DISAPPEARANCE

Nobody peeled the oranges but they open   wings
and carapace   dance on the updrafts   slacken on down
    their musk bright on fingers   moist in the eyes

you are childish   you are so childish   you

think one dead boy replaces another   and if you just
held your breath   you'd become one
    gleamy cold pearl

you are   deep in the municipal pool   gathering nacre
around that word   grit, wound   secreting a shine upon
clasped in breakable lips   will you respond

when   in a voice panicdrunk like a fire alarm
    in swoops your mom   calling and calling you
something wrong   cracks the humectant summer

sky in two   will you make like a tree and

rustle protestuous   split down the middle   cleave
root from rings from branch from quavering
    tendril

    all corpseblossom and loam   where a place
marks a loss   where the crated
oranges dimple and bruise   you are childish

still   in the heart of the pool   you are opening
your eyes where chlorine blue veins shine
radical bright through the water   don't answer

or that will be your real name

AN ACT

Pretending — a tendency tense with presence,

                        tenderness,

                                an end in it:

       to be slim, slick, with skin like skim milk,

only secretly

      sick. It started with the heart, startling it

                    into being a part

            — the art of that

                host of close-woven

                        defenses, the in-

        discernible curtain of fictions drawn to shield

     the girl I killed.

           Still the taint in my certainty

                surfaces churlishly, states

       that if I'm to be held, it will help

to spill only bits of myself,

      to let slip

        a courteous hint

           to convince with my intimacy, or else

     for the sake of a detail I've saved

           to succor me.

                    & if ever a lavish

      fact comes untucked, it must be latched

in the black of a past I can't

      unpack, an ache in the *each* I reach

          for endlessly. The

      faintest fracture in integrity spreads,

unmendable. Best hold still

      and plunge the needle in — let the chemical pen

            cross each X

      out and scribble Y in. Don't

    look down

      on doubt: the no, the now, the ledge

          at the edge

    of knowledge. No one had made any promises I

  would turn out to be someone

I liked.

TRANS PEOPLE OF THE PAST

At some point you must've stood

        stunned in a room and looked

               down at your hands.

           I did that

    once at Eva Burger's kitchen table

        in Ronkonkoma, that windy shoebox house,

     while my mother passed around

        a bucket of fried chicken, and once

    alone in the bathroom afterwards

  to check.

     Did you hide fishnets, stash a hat

        behind a shelf of sheets? Material feels

     a way when forbidden. Slip it on

like a luscious idea — I can picture the seam

        beneath your fingers, skin's echo against

   mute cloth.

  How could anyone know you?

      Carving your privacy

        out of the days like meat

   from an opened animal. Choosing the right

knife —

   the thought that lets

     you have existed

        before. Did you make yourself think it

    over and over? When

       one person unbuttoned your shirt in a wavery

   act of belief, were there words

     for the body you were?

The seam spread across everything jealously

                               fast, kept the former flesh

             close. What's a border

if not an attachment

              staked in revulsion? That dirt is my dirt,

                         my skin

has a pinkish color. Under the lightbulb dangling a long cord

                       down from the ceiling,

                              I

                saw myself like I had never

        met me before. Reluctant to lift

a fist to the display case

         of my life, with a placard marked COMMON ANCESTOR

                            I stood still

              behind — did you feel that? Like

   everyone else was exemplary: the white boy

         in the apple tree, the girl in patent leather loafers; watch

     them radiate, cluelessly,

grace,

     trading card saints ablaze on the promise

            of god? God, *I* want to burn

and not notice, feel the flame breathe in me, float

          on what I know

             and know. But I had to

      reenter that tooth-colored kitchen, the *in situ*

             tableau of preparations

     to continue: potatoes sloshed into

GladWare, thighs sealed skintight

       with Saran — the prayer, preserve us

             in immigrant stillness,

         strung

    bead-like on the generator's hum

we're here   we're here   we're

            here —

               and not shatter, not disappear,

                       since the boy I'd first

            glimpsed in my hands in the yellowish

light would die with me unless

            I could stitch his

                  genesis to your erasure,

                         the syntax the suture

THE CIVIL SURGEON

Didn't agree with me on my eye color.
I said it was more chestnut, and he wrote *beer*
the way when you tell someone else to look up
at a particular star
     you can't be sure
it is your constellation at which they are nodding,
even if their breath is warm on the curve of your
ear, and you want to believe in the trusty
abstractions again.
    The air
was like entering after hysterically laughing
a room where a third person silently
lies. I had dreams of a voice saying, *Each*
question will be repeated twice
and only twice,
     unless
you retake the test.
Retake the test.
    Woke up with the sweats
and then I came here, carrying a picture
of who you should be seeing when you
look at me in my head. It was heavy
like the slosh of a toilet flushed endlessly
into the night,
    obsessive, obsessive,
because if love is domination I just want
to be collected: hung
     askew & loved

for the stutter my color makes in a room's
hum of time. Well, you can't always be
who you were in that other room
here. I've kept this fact for years,
                          a splinter
dark and harmless as a carp under the surface of
my skin. Sometimes I feed it hopeful
imagery:
            I picture myself living
back when no one imagined the earth as an ending
thing, on a raft with a nuclear briefcase
trying to relax, to forget the vast, unjustified
destructions I have in me
                          to enact.
I wanted to tell him I wanted
to pass. There's nothing wrong with me
visible.
        But just
stuck out my tongue, going over the statement
I'd make if we spoke the same language.
                              I'd ask,

Will you still send me back if you
don't assume I was home? I'd say
like an empty can
to the hand that held me,
                    You think
when you throw something away
you throw it away

BROTHER

I know that He exists.

Somewhere — in silence —

—Emily Dickinson (365)

I.

Went away someone. At some point deeply, completely
wordless, unpersoned, husk of a burning-
all-night-long boat cupping dawn's discreetly
blushstruck sky. Has a habit of turning
each action into foreshadowing, loss does. Pulpits
resonate as threats get made yet rosewood
balustrades distract us; questions — was the culprit
pleasure? negligence? genetics? or could
one indict the callow stickyfingered
hand of fate? — obsess. Yes, went away
the sun a boy was but the moon of him lingered,
lingered and grew, since vacancy can stay
gibbous a long time — part wall, part projection,
flooding my blood with its cold light, this language infection.

II

Memories, what memories? Mom's plastic
comb carved whorls in our dark-wet hair, hasty
and fierce on tangles; every toaster pastry
cracked with scalding jelly; every drastic
diagnosis boxed you up with new
instructions: who you were, what you might do
or never would. Unopened as a stone,
you sat cross-legged, rocking towards the wall.
You overheard it, understood it all,
our childhood. Or else I was alone.

III.

Went inside, did he, and where was *inside*?
Didn't have no doors, stood without window
ever, ever open. Tried naming his emptiness, tried
to measure it in hopes the honeyslow
vowels would flow in thick slurred drips
like they once did. A crust covers over whatever
glistens inarticulate. Caught in his lips,
the press of a plosive forever
unexploded — a negative judgment sealed tight
against us, or unactivated love?
How much of a person is in there right
now? How much is he — are *we* — devoid of,
standing pressing every button here
over and over at him like a door might appear?

IV.

Field of your language, a shudder runs through it,
hesitant obstruent, penitent slice of a sigh's
clumsy scythe. Each time a fresh stalk stood, it
bowed when one gust cut it down to size,
broke. Crumbled underfoot, dispersing
brittle spikelets, word-seeds crushed inside,
your sentences grew less and less a person's
excrescences, and more the petrified
chaff of a lost season. I can't harvest
those dry stutter-cuttings for a meal,
however hard I hunger. They're the farthest
field from nourishment until I feel
your hands on my shoulders dismantle the fantasy you
are not a boy but a landscape grief breathes through —

V.

Responds to own name: always, sometimes, <u>rarely</u>,
never. Initiates cooperative play:
always, sometimes, rarely, <u>never</u>. Barely
reacts to stimuli (loud sounds, pain). Stays
still for less than: <u>1 minute(s)</u>. Aggressive
tendencies towards self (head-banging, hitting, biting): <u>yes</u>.
Aggressive against others: <u>rarely</u>. Demonstrates expressive
capacities in cases of: <u>attention-seeking, fear, protest,</u>
<u>demand</u> (Mother reports he takes her hand
and uses it to reach desired objects).
Demonstrates imagination: <u>no</u>. Speech is more/<u>less</u>
complex than last year's, <u>more</u>/less difficult to understand.
Makes eye contact: sometimes, <u>rarely</u>, never.
Will stay this way: for now, for years, <u>forever</u>(?)

VI.

We put gates up in the house to keep
you from us. But your voice leapt the railing,
ringing its one scream into our sleep
as if you were some god we kept on failing
thanks to our hopeless ignorance and
softness. We couldn't sit up like you, wrist
raised to chin, back straight, spit-dripping hand
cupped to mouth, and shout and shout. We missed
when you stopped being you, and now your sound
hollows us out — that loud keened vowel — eight
seconds away, always. Since then, I've found
that bland blank face as your hands shook the gate
follows me, its moonwhite cheeks concealing
how that scream felt. Did you have a feeling?

VII.

Jealous, yes. Of the all-day reality TV
marathon your strangeness made you star of —
each syllable or spit bubble, each recognizably
human gesture captured, praised. I starved.
Could one of your blond guest star therapists
please place *my* dumbstruck fingers on her lips
and say with great precision, *boy*? I raged
that you could care less for the battles waged
to raise the doctors' ratings of your future;
that you controlled us by not speaking ever,
while I, unasked-for savior, strove to suture
our narratives together yet dissever
our natures; that, *sans* you, I'm undefined,
but you're complete: a mind unmined. Not mine.

VIII.

Don't worry, don't worry, this is all routine —
you're white children, these are the suburbs, and money
is gonna flood Daddy's lap so fast it's not even funny
with one more quarter in that slot machine;
these stacks of red, white, and blue chips can be
redeemed for months of private therapy
to make you talk, a necklace to placate
the wife, a lease on that life we were meant
to own — yet doubts like debts proliferate
when I consider how your words are spent.

IX.

There must be a replacement warranty,
or have attempts to fix this person rendered
it void? Where is our money back guarantee,
good for a lifetime? I can't feel tender
recognition at the thin whiteblue
scar above your eye from when you broke
my window on your face. I don't know who
this person is, much less how to revoke
our love, dispute the charge, cancel the check,
when once it seemed the mechanism ran
flawlessly, just as it had been sketched:
a boy who could be made into a man,
and not gray teeth ground to a rusty pause,
this cracked case, the eraser smudge your voice was.

X.

I dreamed your death so many times: the peel
of skin slicked off, the fruit-rot of your seizing
cerebellum splattered into viscous purple jewels
on concrete, or the gasp, thrash, dirt-clutch, heaving
drown, plastic wrap to the mouth, the chalice
and electric orange vomit on your lime
green shirt, or else the curt decisive slice
of the carotid, throbbing, the surprised
look, the relinquish — your sprawled frame
now folded like a switchblade back within
its case: age, cause of death, sex, name —
but when I grasp the coffin's sides, look in,
resemblance is a corpse I can't outpace,
my open eyes locked fast in our closed face.

XI.

You loved him like a saint or an animal, Mother.
Thought his love purer than mine. Well, fine.
Back of his stare, like a candle, *something* was
burning — distance with no name, no border
we could see. On nights when, unexpectedly,
one clear word of human language leaves
his mouth, it could make you believe
for a moment, couldn't it? Make you grasp his
image in the tendrils of your brain and hold on.
I am doing it. I am still holding
this negative burned to expose the corners
of who else my brother might have been —
even now, I color its lovingness in
like stained glass, and yet I have doubts, Mother.

XII.

According to the pictures, we were kids
with loose gold ringlets, cheeks like custard cream,
the works. But when I used to watch you dream,
your warm eyes shut beneath your cold eyelids,
your limp fist curled quiescent, I could sense
this was the closest we would ever be —
you only as far from the word as an ordinary
boy asleep. Your breaths were recompense
for all the days I'd made myself believe,
despite the fits, the fists, the wrecks, the shrieks,
you might have peace. That blond boy wakes and speaks
to me from photographs — my sweet unless,
my past perfective. Once you've left, you leave
a hush that swells in me like childlessness.

XIII.

Should I have been you. Born with a silence
curled inside you like the end of breathing,
beating your wrists on the wall with no concept of violence,
hearing our words with no means of believing
they mean. Love, opened if I did a letter
for some other boy meant, deeply I
apologize. Stole if I did — a debtor
pocketing a rich mind's keys — your eyes'
luster, your tongue's nimbleness, for keeps,
you won't (won't you) forgive me, brother?
If I usurped the voice in you that sleeps,
unresurrectable, and with another
ghost replaced it — cutpurse necromancer
that I've become — your absence is my answer.

XIV.

Did I become a boy because our father
wanted one but ended up with you?
Full-breasted, thick-hipped, cake-faced, five-foot-two,
I had some work to do to be another
person. Once by knifelight, being dead
seemed like a streamlined answer to the vast
genetic accident we'd both been cast
to play in drag — I straightlaced, you undone.
When I told him I was a man, he said,
I have *a son*.

XV.

You've changed. Grown — not *up* but somehow
into. Into what? A broad, soft-shouldered
silence, ever deeper. Even now
your stare submerges every minder. Older,
profounder each year, though your tongue is still
a two-year-old's, and your brain eight or nine,
according to the tests. I'll wait until
you've watched the cartoon shipwreck twenty times
with no sound, on rewind, before I try
to say goodbye. Each time it reassembles
the shattered hull and all its flames subside,
your spine sticks straight up and your left hand trembles,
expectant. What you wreck, you memorize —
like love. My drowned face wavers in your eyes.

XVI.

Summer, another. This time you're not under
a comforter sweating your brains out in blistering heat
with no fan and the aide out on the street
taking an hourlong smoke break. I still wonder
how many seizures no one took down, how
those mysterious bruises showed up on your throat,
your breadsoft arms. We got you out; we wrote
complaints, threats. How should I protect you now?
If I can be your keeper through these seasons
of sunshine and slow death, my drugged-up slack
spaceshot savant, my source, my curse, my freak
accident remnant, my hieroglyph, all my reasons,
teach me to believe you love me back.
I'll listen. You don't need to speak.

XVII.

Good
Work
Hi go in car
For walk for swimming
Listen music Watch a tape Say
Supercalifragilisticexpialidocious
Little Mermaid Peter Pan go in
car Market Pretzels Orange juice
In car swimming Chickenchicken coop
Say
I love to laugh
I want go Out
I love you
Matthew

THERE

Я забыл существованье,
я созерцал
вновь
расстоянье.
—Александр Введенский, «Гость на коне»

I forgot existence,
I beheld
anew
distance.

—Aleksandr Vvedensky, "Ghost on Horse"

TIME TO DESTINATION

My happiness is vast: there's distance in it. It's, from the plane, the atmosphere-unobscured
view of the landscape of — soon — arrival, the greenness of high summer and squat
humblegold bales in fields, almost invisible, and the periphery — clustered houses, some
derelict, some pristine, hard to see — on identical plots, then the scrapyards,
milk factory, chicken processing plant, fulfillment center, and the tracks,
their slow rush below us into the city, the city — big buildings rise in the windows, suddenly
we are here. The joints in my fingers click shut like tiny Swiss Army knives
and a lemonlime neon light threads round my edges, pulses a soft fluorescence,
and this cardboard cutout of me, almost weightless, floats against the black of endless space —

briefly

til the whole screensaver galaxy deluges into me, filling me all heavy-empty like
true rhyme. If today is my life,
let it be an animal with calm eyes and a dusky muzzle
bending towards my open hand, gently. Let me press my face into his buckskin shoulder
and weep, or just breathe, like: I know him, I've trained him,
I know how to break him — or else let me never land
in that field of hours where he stands, all statuesque and mortal — let me hover, scared
he won't recognize me, and this place won't be home because home
doesn't exist, and will he still carry me where I need to go? It's the maybe

that keeps me

DRONE PASTORAL

Negev Desert, 2011

Everyone had the same question
relating to death and what needed to happen
in the name of rain. Where was our myth

like a weir to dam the stream of contingencies
threatening everything inch by inch or sometimes
quicker, sucking all the one-word answers under

and leaving their shells to barnacle in the sediment
all along a month, twelve months, a generation?
Leave them there. We wanted air —

the ground seen from it, curve
of a face turning slowly away from the light,
tame as we had not known it. Pliable and just

waiting for its coordinates, for some vast power
to master the shape of it, throw down a net
and own it. The desert resembles

nothing so much as a screen: each particulate
pixel holds this settlement, this dead-letter
empire together under the phosphate quarry's

radioactive ash. A promise is
immaculate, unlike an act
which is why I have brought you here,

because in the heat of it, heart of its
crude-blazing center, the city distracts
itself from the nature of water. Now

there are no lights to put out;
the night's bark grows over the mouth
of each house in its hushed distinction,

over the once-forest, dust, over us children
tangled in the leafery of stars all whispering,
There are hosts in the absences, listen

TARKOVSKY

[indistinct chatter]
say the subtitles, and my
eyes listen harder

tug the loose thread of
sadness through the syllables
the familiar

fray where the voice's
poise starts to
unravel — swallowed

vulnerability
like a stone in the throat
of the broken-faced

former bus driver
onscreen — because his dream
to hoist his past and leave

the only city
he has known evacuates
me. I can feel the

last thread snap, then drop.
Then a silence: the kind of
day when the sun seems

to carve light into
every edge, a medieval
engraver with gold

leaf stuck to fingers
that have traced each frontispiece
since the birth

of the world. A hard
reverential light
as if the day watched

what becomes of us.
In this movie, it does: it
lavishes the man

with attention nothing else
pays — his misgivings, mistakes.
It is based on real life.

TOMSK MON AMOUR

Siberia was suicide with a view, an inhabitable
                              abstraction. God, I wanted so much to be cold
in the air of an answer. Freely I clambered
                    up creaky steps to the bell tower and clutched
the heavy rope — breathed hard and felt
                 time. Fast, after a long hesitation: that
was how I did things then. Struck awake but
                   dully, with a foreigner's fish-eyed stupidity,
sockets stocked with consciousness,
             too much. Its granules clung
to the folds of my brain like sweet
            coffee powder clotted on the ridges
of a flimsy plastic cup whose scald
            still haunts. I lived in the morning,
which crossed — like a railroad — everything
              in a way that made it someplace else.
Need connects. Then an afternoon comes:
            all cheekbone and graffiti over brickwork
built by convicts — arctic air, and her
           in a wool hat eating an ice cream bar.
The Madonna of Stalingrad, she said,
          was sketched in charcoal in a trench
on the back of a soldier's map of Russia, nothing
          to lean against. It was the most
I've ever loved someone I just met. The word *moment*
         is мгновение — it lasts four syllables and first emerged
from a verb, now lost. How small can one
         be broken down? When I was deleted,

street names blew through me, whole villages

                               of nobody, the colorful trim on shacks

like fatal eggs. Crouched in the female

                    body's foxhole, pockets full of the dead,

the cold coins of their faces, I

               had agreed to survive. *But guilt is a debt,*

the wind said, *and the debtor's corpse will know*

                    no peace. To be someone's replacement

explicitly — to breathe a stranger's air — is

                  a poison, a gift. To have left and grown rich

with absences. *Know me only a little,*

               I wanted to tell her, *and you'll get me better,*

for once I was nameless, for once I was paper

                   back when I lay on the blank field, a hyphen

          promising

STREET OF THE FRIENDSHIP OF NATIONS

Siberia, 2010-2011

I.

You, on a tiny white stool knee-deep
in sedge grass in a crunchy shearling coat
as the clouds drift nearer — winter

again, as children clamber
screamingly atop the gas pipe in their mucky parkas
to burst from it like loud, chromatic blooms,

what would you give for a view of
your plot from above: the one son gone
to the war, and the younger shooting

krokodil into his arm, the elbow's
crook where once the infant nestled in her pink
skin, where every summer, mother

earth yields up, moronically, acres of radioactive cucumber,
where now the clang of the blacksmith's hammer drowns
beneath the rush of Moscow women's voices

caterwauling on *Let's Marry!*
on Lyuba the neighbor's TV (grainy, angry) —
would not it be interesting for you

to see how the puddle of oil alongside
the tracks glints up at the thawed sky
like insight, land surveying its own face

through some drone's eyes?

II.

Fate's a hologram, the light of each
possible outcome of one life diffracted
across a field of interferences

whose surface lets just one shape shine
out at a time. Viewed in parallax,
this could be both of us —

we could be pushing
a babypink carriage through the gustiest layer
of that jar of sun and dust cloud, Sebastópol,

our tan faces blown
featureless and the red roofs, the red roofs
blurred behind us and the sands like God's

cast-off fatigues spread untrodden ahead,
the horizon so huge it looks almost
demilitarized —

but you and I
shimmer on the mirror's edge
betwixt this lake and that full-color

hunger. Can you remember
anything actually terrible,
the kind of event folks unfolding

newspapers would see, clutch
their coffees involuntarily
with feeling? We were absent, yes,

we continue our absence
from famines, mass executions — a phrase like *the border*,
spectral until concretely

thrown up against an escape. Our fate
is to have faces and catch them abstracted
here, in this coppery green, scum-crusted lake

— unbloody, undistorted —
and of which nobody,
not even us, takes a picture

III.

Shut up, I don't want to know

                        what our rights are — faces pressed to glass

                        as the bus cantankers westwards
                        through a long, green yawn of exurb,

breaths condensing,
petal droplets gasp against cellophane as
the blade makes its distinction —

                        passing crossed-out village names:
                  Sugarhead, Shoelaces, Cursed Hump, Desire

here

no one talks about fame and why should they,
eighty kilometers and a day's wages in gas

                        to go stand on the street where the banks are,
                        picking at your scalp. But that one place

where I and future casualty three-thousand-nine-hundred-thirty-eight sat
sliding the chunks of meat off the charred
skewers with our fingers, the ketchup perfectedly

red, we weren't drunk but free

                            enough. Dima's grand schemes, the grease in his laugh

IV.

What does the caption *a decaying barn* communicate,
ramshackle in a field of unpronounceables that poke

up like stalks in spring turf, all the small,
cold-sounding places? What do the horse's

blackened knees and snout and sweaty withers,
the blinders coarse against his eyes,

represent? Who even knew
there was a border there? *It runs,*

he says, *through my potato plot.*
I cannot till it now.

V.

White bodies are lying on the ground in dark coats — four white bodies.
Make that five. All sprawled out unseemly, puddled in cheap felt, in folds
on a corner of Nevsky. Rain sloshes the cobbles, this deafening thin-
scrim-of-the-world-coming-down-all-around sound. My eyeballs are cold, my feet
are too far away. I am a stain on a white background, and the gray
walls press towards my back. Come in. I used to have a fear
of background, but now you are all I ever wanted.

VI.

You get to be in the picture, and you get to
stay there. Let some scholar translate your stare

into the usual what-are-you-doing-here,
let his assistant and all his successors close your eyes

in the first of two leather-bound volumes. You
do look surprised, so many years later,

so many years dead — exposure
without protection from its effects

still shocks, I guess. It's so intimate, helpless
in what it gives up to the light: your bony

forearms, your feet thick with mud, your britches
rolled up past white knees, and the tight

fear in your squint. Is to stare to possess
you, *Peasant Boy, Odessa* —

you exact fantasy, you embossed copy
of an irrecoverable self? I was like you

when I was your age,
authentic. Then one of us got to be somebody else.

VII.

Nomadic people have lost most of their
livestock due to drought. I hadn't heard,
had only thought of being one of those girls,
tucking her dark, sleek wave of hair
out of sight. The cotton, the red veil
of road grit always clinging to the cotton,
and the thornless blue dome rising frail
to the east, towards Irkutsk. She says, *It's gotten
hard to learn to read*, to spurn the son
who put his dusty bottle of grape soda
down, slung his long gun over her shoulder,
and promised her a life. Told her no one
in skyscrapers knows where the lies start, or
which guys are infidels. Who wins this war.

VIII.

Who gets to have a late style? The atmosphere, thickening hum
of sunlight pressed between the pane and rustle of translucent curtains,
tangled in embroidered vines fine as the bones of an ear,
or the spoony, green shafts of the houseplant reaching to grasp —

what, exactly?

Nothing in this room is asking what its shine *reminds you of,*
the polyester flowers don't encourage your touch, crisply
unstained by the soil that the people mean when they say *earth,*
and pressed by Shandong Province's
stainless steel hands. Is that flatness,

that lack

of breaks in the lock-stitched hem, synonymous with lateness?
Your dream was the front row seat at the origin story, your dream was to see
the stiff hook of the goose's neck
arch beneath the elbow of the man who has done this before,
has strained under the belly as the feathers turned heavy

before. But

this is not your kitchen. You can perch here on its sill, ornament
from an irrelevant climate, absorbing to your delectation each
crumb with your keen, irrelevant eyes —
and still, what you give up, you give up freely.

It's never *your* life,

unless — late, once night's walls flare shut and you breathe in
a swarm of greasy stars aswim, rippling through the skein that gilds
hot milk — could you be there, yourself and completely, then,
and stand in socks beside the flame that licks the saucepan's base, unlost
in the hiss of its dead blue heaven?

IX.

Imagine a municipal waste facility rich with deposits
of lithium-ion batteries, memory chips, all that immortality
dumped in a pit in the moist dirt out past Khimki, where the river
"walks" each year, late spring — that's what they call it
when the thick ice crust cracks and the floes shudder and crash
their sun-drunken shoulders against each other all the way
to the last moraine.
                                    Just think of the memories
borne on SIM cards through cold, silty water up the Ob
across the floodmeadow, athwart the plots of all possible lives…
somewhere in that clutch of ones and zeroes, a girl hides
her eyes. Somewhere was — maybe still is — a dacha with a garden,
tomatoes and cucumbers glistening after morning rain, the sudden
blur of her ear as she turns her face away not fast enough
from the guy with the black device, who gets
                                                        his shot.

X.

It didn't happen in English, that shift
       from arrival to remaining — absence in the cast-
off ending — he stressed, looking
       over the grease-pocked paper plate, the crust of his
ketchup and mayonnaise pizza, past the shattering-
       slowly door, its cracked glass, fractured star
with glints splintering off, past the trolleybus terminus
       towards the evergreens, like he could see the minute sphere
of melt caught on the tip of each needle of each branch of each
       tree, and cast disdainfully away the temporary

peace. With sun full in his face, he looks wallpapered,
       like a candle saint. How do you say: my grief
is not to be a landscape — not, after four billion years of calm
       and then a crash, an extinction carting its retinue of distractions
flaming across the horizon, still to be here —
       dry under a slicker of millennia as the days rain down,
fixed to witness him from every angle, fluent in sky
       the way a river, swaddled up to its mouth, knows earth
— gladly? Shift, discard the crumpled
       pause, and return to your country

WHERE

When the subject so expands,
does not the object shrink?

—Clifford Geertz, *Works and Lives:*
The Anthropologist as Author

ON DEVOTION

Hello again, my sickness.

                    I can feel you breathing

                                      in the cracks between my bones

like light almost,

                ripping the scrim of my proprioception

                                    stitch by anxious stitch —

what will you whisper into my

                    crevices this time? What ludicrous promise

must the drug make, peeling open every petaled cell

                            with its rain-fingers if

                                        nevertheless

you thirst? You are the only one on earth

                    who wants me completely,

                                    whose tinfoil swaddles each

leftover gesture I lift to read its expiration date.

                              You are the one awake

and throbbing like the nacreous

                    gasoline bleeding its colors into a puddle once the taxicabs

disperse.
>   When the end gusts across us
>   and opens our surface so wide the sky completely

penetrates and fills us with blank blue,
>   I will still hold you
>   as the father holds the blade

against his son's throat, prays
>   for intercession
>   and the stars shine down hard

on all the toxic bloomstruck fields of
>   earth, this consequence.
>   I know no one escapes.

DROUGHT PASTORAL

I wanted you, desert,
your red incorruptible

parchedness perched on
the earth's bone shoulder

songless as the hot
wind soughs through you

and the dump truck windows
gleam like opened blisters

at high noon. Today I
heard the grass growing,

whispering its one shared word
blade to blade until the whole

green lawn knew it. Guilt
seeped up into me droplet

by droplet until morning
cast it off shivering, every

tiny globe. Which lives
and which deaths do I own?

A barrenness
thrives in me;

a flock of toxins feasts
among the Styrofoam

takeout containers my organs,
sprawled in the sun, become.

It happens so slowly —
the kidneys' deliquescence,

the wrists' eight dinky bones
ground to a powder that seeps

into groundwater, granular
as one egg in the slurry

of my womb. To be holy
is not to hope anything

grows from this, I know,
to stand impassive as a cliff's

face, formed when the desert rose
up in grief millennia ago

and not expect
nourishment or resurrection

in a handful of rain.
But I can't stop

bleeding for the future
as the automatic sprinkler

seems to love the curb,
casts its glistening veil

of tears over and over it.
Open up, desert,

and let me down into you
seven thousand feet —

where once the cage stops
shaking I can hear my lungs

breathe — where once
your pleats of rockflesh

clutched a silver seam
for boys like me to rip

and scrape the clots
of bounty out. I want

that dark igneous
solace of just

before they knew what
we had in us.

CRIP ALBUM

I.

Fourteen-year-old girl in power
wheelchair: arm
rests under arms, with head
rest cradling head, with neck
cocked backwards, white, a shot
swan's spine and candlestick
legs and the useless immaculate
shoes (pink Skechers) as the lips
dispatch a rivulet of spit
down the chin. She's sick
of sitting in her own wet. Stuck
in her head, a song by Taylor Swift

II.

Muscular American
veteran, civilian
polo shirt, old IED
glow in his eyes, plastic
basket in his lap in aisle three
— frozen dinners, novelties —
space beneath
each knee

III.

Scoliotic uncle:
kitchen radio speechifying
brimstone as a crumb drops
, bending

IV.

Octogenarian in a lace skeleton,
her blue capillaries are
ivy's conquest of a wall
crumbling from inside. Her eyes
say anyone can have this
latticed bone scantling to
ponder but the plot
thereunder, never

V.

Was I disabled then? Was I ever
disabled later — all shaky achy hunched over
the shaft of the bronze-painted cane with its rubberized foot collecting
sand in the grooves of — for after, for when
none of my legs on that beach would stand

VI.

Juxtaposition isn't
equivalence until
we are objects

VII.

Brown boy,
wiry, rising
from a river. His unsplit
chest gleams wet,
his shield. Every
body's deaf
in pictures

VIII.

still life
with ten
pill bottles
vial &
needle

IX.

Nonplussed teenager
trims bangs of demented
former prize fighter,
shut-eyed under
scissors, who delivers
urgent updates on a bout
from 1973. When he
recognized
the pole, its slowly
twirling stripes the color of
America, what joy

X.

Please complete the form.
Check one:
      ☐ sovereign individual
      ☐ preexisting condition

XI.

Cheerful-seeming, slim
woman in black leather jacket
with two-hundred-thirty-eight-pound legs,
engorged fungus colossus
infected / cut off / sprouting / sprouting — how

you look to her
(not pictured)

XII.

Not pictured:
invasive species
burgeons in thoracic
swamp. All night
a fine chemical rain
falls in the dark of this body

XIII.

Staircase in my house I can't
what *story* once meant neutrally
no help no entry needing proof no
clamber drunk up to the roof
on someone else's voice pain-
less epiphany healed cut sealed
shut skylight no other country

XIV.

Look, it's the mute
boy again. Thin, clean,
impish in between
ice cream and seizure —
the blur is his twitch.
See the scar on his fist?
Cut the big mirror
open, reflectionless.
The blood from his vein
is the rain's conversation
promising, promising
him the garden's
soft and wordless dirt,
for all you know

XV.

Hey kid, what if you spoke?

XVI.

Self-portrait:
two-months-premature,
four-pound newborn
girl is perfect. Nothing
wrong with her.

INFUSION SUITE PASTORAL

I have my fears and I have let them go
painstakingly as summer its last leaf —
that one to the left, chrome yellow
flecked with umber, drifting towards a patch
of stale toast grass that wants

to be done now. Watch it land with me,
casually — look how the invisible
breeze that must've been lifting it up
just enough after each rush earthward stops.

As if to drop were effortless! For years,
I've been trying to peel the slick clear
plastic backing of prognosis off the stubbornly
resilient adhesive of old hopes. But we were
manufactured together — one future

and one boxed-in body inextricable as nature
is from the ghost of my face on this extra clean
vitrine. The glare makes its assertion:
you can get only so close to the earth,

no closer, can carry yourself like a glass of water
full to the brim up a red rock escarpment to where
the dirt waits to be slaked — and discover
nothing you touch it with heals. This distance
breeds in me a cruelty, a steady

induration, all the layered pains and hatreds
stiffening like icebox cake; it makes
even the lushest cusswords curdle on my tongue.
I'm young! And not that sick — I can persist for years

like this. The suite has all one needs to stay
docile as the air in an empty cage,
still as The Past seems to stand in its armature
of dates and facts. But nerve endings remember
touching you like it might give me our life back,

like — if only I could get down on my knees in the grass,
feel the gravel of centuries pressed to my bones
and no pain at all, *no pain at all* — I'd melt into the mutual
world again, with its food court smoothie stands,
brutalist county jails, harvest festivals

celebrating bees, with the smell of wet train tracks
crossing a dawn, irreproducible —
and on the bench someone actually laughing
at a second person's joke.

That's my last fear: not to be here. Already
I feel myself leaking attention
in rivulets I can't trace back to some source
of meaning. Already the station clock's stopped
glowing for me like a place we would get to eventually,

and the spry, healthy denizens of the vending machine
are my enemies. I so want to resemble them
it's beyond forgiveness — fractureless
as I pretend they are in their skins, their beliefs....

Is that what the pastoral is? Lust
to read yourself into a landscape you're not sure
exists anymore? To pump the old colors back
into it like spring, repapering the trees until
even this year's damage seems

natural — to rip out the needle and stand
cold on the lawn in a paper gown as the stars burn
exactly where our folktales told them to,
shining with all the indifference of proof
on the questions they close, then reopen?

STRANGERS

Poverty isn't spiritual,
he said and took a mouthful
on his fork. The evening was all black and blue,

tinged with Dos Equis around the edges,
the air warmer than I was used to. Out
of fear, I seldom hope. When I enter

a church of the New World, I catch myself
holding my breath for a sec, you know?
It's like that: you meet someone

and the day starts to shed its protection
to stick to the wound, poised over

the distance between. That cool stale air,
smell of stone, and those old women

filling it with their belief, candle-flicker
threaded through it — *We are evil,*
someone loves us.

He said it was a desert
rife with gunshots. I listened:
he didn't say anything else.

When we fucked, later later
I felt the condom between us, too,
like a truncated plot. The casualty

tracker rose faster. *Inside me*, I ordered.
Dead, dead, dead.

As he came, he made a face like pain,
and I felt empathy then.

THE CENTER

I hate travelling and explorers.
—*Claude Lévi-Strauss*, Tristes Tropiques

So much sun we can't see nothing. A squint: it won't question but fasten
                its look on the nearest & sink tiny eyelashhooks into it,
    disappear distance. Is this what a camera does
                better than us, hum the gaze's approximant —
not precise / not turbulent, a frictionless continuant —*yes* or *west*
    exemplars of it — til the shutter's teeth
                                click shut? But here we are, wind
        rakes through our
                            breathspetals, cold plunderer. The sky a ransacked color,
cautiously cloudless with a chance of loss. & this thing called The State,
            where is it? Blurred, how the trash fires shimmer
                a million small, a slow sweet reek of rubber rising
                                                        as flies ride its updrifts
                        abuzz with a gossip so fulsome it's gathered the everywhere air of
Fact. Pothole / cobblestone / telephone pole
                                    / stickfigure citizen X
                                            -ed out, none of which needs
                                                    Look, it's
to watch us very carefully. Stares make a fastidious consequence.
            the center: its white buildings repainted whiter, pair of self-righteous
                                            traffic lights & the national hero

bronze-browed, square-shouldered, appraising the future

behind a staid hedge of impatiens.

Have we ever heard of him?

Have these women in puffy skirts, wheeling across the plaza's raucous gravel

carts stacked with shelf on shelf of jiggling

cherry jello, each with a snow foam dollop

in his *adidas* sweatsuit & lightning-bolt haircut, heard?

of real cream — has the kid with the fistful of spoons,

Since a square is not history. History gets

to meander distractedly with a notebook & no sense of direction & collect

a watch / a stench / a pink church with

inscriptions to be translated later by dictionary, because authenticity

must be invented. Every impurity, every mass-produced

candy bar or souvenir; ought to get airbrushed out — & the awkward

genocide origin-story, the rush as conquistadors swarm across a forgiveless

bewilderness, each out to claim his plot —

a marble fountain, scarless, could be built on that, calmly to plash

the same anthem over & over. History can't

even hear itself blink, but each cut makes an edition — complete

continent-portrait: desert

with full-color map & the old capital

demoted from bold to italic. That's

the Political, then there's the Physical

sprawls across the landsflesh like a rash. Could we approach

the intimacy of black ink that bleeds into the green / can we

cling like the hard fur of dirt to the brickwork / are we

as close to the place as that?

To embrace the chilled parfait of centuries like a gasp

of plastic wrap, to seal in all the details, was my dream:

to take

the frosted glass from the display case — I confess —

home with me. Replace

each verb I won't own up to, every name my lips can't taste,

the false I was. In its stead, to instate

some tin-roofed rusting bungalows or else

a pawn shop, an opera house, so late that now even the women

lined along the boulevard are rolling up their huge blue tarps awaiting

the last bus — with nods to the others — *yes, goodnight* —

as neon stains their cheeks. At the hour when each

building is nobody's, like the moon

that bathes the cobblestones until each pebble is laved to the shine

of a lake's black face, when a sinister boringness hangs

over streets like the smell of hospital on my sick skin, I can

see our having-come for what it was: a hunt

for half-garbled echoes, born out of synonym lust, of a rush for the place

to undress its premises, the way the red & gold fried chicken signs blaze their greasepromise

sleeplessly into all night until they are the blur

of one great hunger. We came to the center

to be an obstacle the light must hit /

a stem

to which some pollen of the whole earthly spectacle sticks.

For the landscape to look at us

as I thought God would once. But the actual visual is a provisional, hurls up partitions like thick

which frays under fat colors / sags /

sheets on our tauttrembling clothesline — *focus* —

snaps. & leaflike

a detail not flagrant enough

to be pressed into memory drifts

away from us so softly it's not even loss

but just forgiveness of a debt we owed the universal

mortgage lender of experience. Since who even *are* we to be here

gathering blisters, nostalgic for something

not-ours? Did we come to bask in uncontagious

indigence, to feel our white

cut holes in the thin construction paper of

these mauve / blood / aqua / bastard-amber buildings as we pass?

No, amigos, no

the woman in braids calls out

& shakes both clodthick hands at us, who — descending

ache-laden, sun-blistered into the valley

with only a camera & a field of turbid sinkholes spread

glistering between our feet & hers — have come many hours, from over the hills,

past the donkeys trundling bottles of red Fanta up the cliffside, past

the furious shrubbery, past the short dusty boy with the whip,

to her village & ask her

for water.

She is brusque, correct. The day flares wide behind her with the silence

the sky keeps when it listens to itself. A few shacks down,

75

tinny synth pop blurts out from behind the fence — a party,

certainly, with loud glad children — & the doused fields glisten. A cow drools.

It struck me only

halfway through the long walk back that I had always wanted that

slap: to be caught /

called out

/ told off.

& after

The everyday does have its price. You can only pay it

once, in one jurisdiction, with one kind of rain

smeared on the plastic picnic tables, those denizens &

resemblances. It is not to notice

how the crows hatch their conspiracy on the industrial bakery lawn,

how enormous is the car the little blonde girl enters, how dentless,

how the days wake & sleep until they are years.

how do you say to someone: *listen,*

this was our cream cheese, this was a VCR, here is a chair

we had to leave behind? How to hold it

It was not condescension

led us to descend, then, but a love

up to another — dripping with dailiness like a rinsed lettuce, one crisp headful

of pure meaning, unexportable?

based on fragmental intel gleaned from Xeroxed reams of travel

guidebooks — streaks of ink across the peaks' facsimile, the elder's face —

the false crossed out but not erased. We came for the actual /

the gauche accidental

intimacies of a country incompletely

ready for us, leaking quiddities from the edges

of its most touristic districts, agape like a house that doesn't

realize where its door is. A shift in political

grammar & now we can enter its living

room—two uninvited mutes, fingering the rims of teacups, breathing particulate air — & hear

inhabitants start to pronounce it.

Sure, I want in — but there's comfort

to listening ununderstandingly, as to a river's pilgrimage towards its mouth

where freighters suck shore's udder & replays of capital's

spectacles air everywhere at once — as every storefront flaunts

knockoff answers to a call the operator drops.

Here with a fake Coke & plate of "Friend potatoes,"

is there some way to participate?

Even at home, I hadn't. I'd configured

my body not to betray me — *hush, stay here*

where they can't see you — & inevitably someone

was standing there with a leotard I had to enter. You know how it is:

& you just can't.

large pale hands, glimpsed through an excess of distance, insist —

They see themselves in you. They keep trying to make you dance

to a music that doesn't exist. Fifty-First Street's no better:

every pedestrian's playing a chess game & you don't remember

which way to glide — or were you supposed to jump over?

Tactical maintenance of an interior

hence becomes essential — here are my tendons, here my separate lungs —

DO NOT ENTER.

The center
was me with my camera: black box raised
to shield my face, squint pressed to sensor,
pupil to sighthole, index cocked to trigger
release of the mirror:

I was the tower the royal cartographer
had to scale to cast his net of named streets over this ramshackle cluster
of shanties / horse-drawn carts / the slow daylaborers
hauling Tuckahoe marble up from the Hudson block by block
for the sake
of a turgid & cakelike cathedral. I stopped on its steps
to text, & the tourists who captured me there,
going about my business gumchewingly with a limp & resentment in my eyes,
for those folks what did I — the passerby,
the native — exemplify?

Was I a splotch upon
the postcardperfect midday midtown sweep of cabs & pretzelvendors, Cartier Henri Bendel
Louis Vuitton Bergdorf Goodman Apple Microsoft Armani Prada Gucci Lord & Taylor Saks?
What words had they all packed
to compass this, & was my purpose just
to be a symptom, to confirm their diagnosis
of excess as disease endemic to the West—thus to attest
their spiritual paths still pointed true, if anxious, North?
The most reverent, pilgrims and penitents, make no maps
& so we are left, it would seem, with an X

-marks-the-spot, the ol' Dig-Here-for-Oil, or else
the jetlagged transcendences: detail — epiphany / detail — epiphany
— not based on talking to anyone, really,
but dazzling as an ectoplasm splashily extruded into the breathless
dark of few facts. No, the language we carried
squeaked like a foot in a large galosh,
never quite right for the task. The excess
words — coriander / assiduous / sunder — swelled with the presumptous
need of the kid who shows up to the field trip with a big bag like somebody might
ask him to stay the night. But when the other boys all speechless
pass the soccer ball between
their bodies red to red to green to
shin to cleat a sinuous
& shifting mesh whose fibers cross
pull tight to stop or loosen knots
& intercept, cleanly release
the toss the kick to arc it
back to center — every part
hurts.
Like something personal but worse
because you know it isn't, wasn't even custom-
made for you. Banal generic total
coat of an unsharable
disease, its too-long sleeves
dragging all over that ground the old anthems
called common.

No way to summon

the crunch of astroturf beneath your cleats back & no needle's-

eye to thread the instant pleasure of the pass — completed —

through. No way to crop your blotchpink finger

out of its perch on the edge of the picture. No

way to be absent except absolutely.

& that, more than anything else, would be

poverty:

not to live / in a physical world.

I'll carry

it with me then, this toppled dictatorship of a body

now rebuilding itself as a shaky democracy — all bonescaffolding & self

-doubt, all its imported hormones, all its unreliable

utilities & walls graffitied with words of the old regime —

my home. Slide the glass into place until it clicks & squint: the metal clips

hold it to the light, fleshfragment

whose cells are fortified cities seen from the air;

each one a smearblur of violet duct cells lining the pink collagenous walls the streams

snake round to bear their protein-rich

juice to the islets. Each nucleus,

miniscule-dark

like a single pedestrian, how its edges sharpen as the knob turns, the objective

homing in — to sluice ravines between them. The cracks always

inside. Unstained,

the islets gape like net's holes & remind

you something leaks through every echo, every rhyme

& doesn't disappear but can't — like the sky around / within / behind

the knots in twine — be caught a second time. Only the dirt

swallows every last particle, every pure pain-granule, & clutches

the cold to its heart like a secret indifference, overhearing

everything / repeating

only its adamant grammar of surface &

the hole that opens, listens

with so fathomless a patience you can't help but tell it all.

HERE

Death was a process then, a release of nostalgia
Leaving you free to change.

—Jon Anderson, "In Sepia"

VANTAGE POINT

Just because I study feelings
doesn't mean I've had them

all, you might've said, but thought
I would come empty-handed

better, two of us like children out
for apples trusting there would be

riper fruit higher, climbing
higher to behold the vast flat sheet of

sky cut up, the branches giving
it a new immensity and them

a view of neighboring
sheaves of grain unnumbered

as dust motes in one beam of sun,
and scintillant as the instant

you gain a belief — so you
offered me the benefit

of the doubt I knew:
there is no wisdom

in these things, each one a one-time blossom cultivated not

only to be pressed between the pages
of two ages but envisioned

as a blur of pollen
uplifted on infinite miniscule

wings and then wind-scattered, drifting
down and downward, softly taking

hold under earth's flesh to be
a part of the measure of things,

a hum in the fat dappled animal
late afternoon, until you can't

tell it from the light and you
wouldn't want to, the kind

of still point we climb up and up
to find, though sure in nature it

never, only with extreme
rarity, arrives — that tight joy I

felt when you kissed the fine
blue roots beneath my skin

and you said *you* to me
like the name of a place.

CLOISTER

Our bodies are about other people.
                              One line of music, illegible,
            encircles your hairy ankle.
                        You suckle, not gentle, at my
    post-surgical nevermind —
                              and what that ache equals, I've
  racked the fucked archives to find.
                        Picnic blanket unscrolling sunlight
          on our excerpt of park.
                              (Accuracy, surprise.)
          Soft smear of
                              mayonnaise, cold cuts bit into, crumbs on a napkin, names.
You showed me, each hand plays
                        more than one voice.
                                    Now you say
          hands and I see yours:
        only, in particular,
                        our hurts the same height,
  similar in what they cast outside.
                        What pattern, then, could you live
          in forever?
                        What unspoken order,
  what just-upon-waking-up dream
                              of transparency?
    (Frosted mylar, damp sheet.)
                        All your hunger
      thrown down like a test —
                        ink it in me.

The tapestry's caption reads

                                  The Unicorn at Rest, but he's

      bleeding. Look, his white neck

                          the repetitive flowers against.

     Pain's its own kind of weather:

meaningless

       depth in a world made for flatness, deadpan as clouds on canvas — yet

across you reached and

           pushed away my crutch. *Here* you *are,*

     said your eyes.

           (Says art.)

              I was literally touched.

BLUE SCREEN PASTORAL

The system has encountered an error
from which it cannot recover

but god it was beautiful, restarting and
restarting —
                dawn cracking open

an eggshell of cloud as the shriek
of the brakes of the first rusty tram of

the day spilled out.
                It was cold: the sound
          hung in the air a long time

like an unbroken vow, a historical
age whose vacancies flickered, snowflake-like

        before drifting earthward, condensing
into future.
        If I had religion

it would be this fissure
rent in the day by the sudden

collision of iron with
                breath — that heavy-empty
pause in which each sedimentary

stratum of anticipation, of action,
hangs, distinct yet connected, like weather

       inside a rock.
 If you had not
uttered the fatal exception that triggered

 the nonmaskable interrupt,
 the timeout signal, the memory dump,

how could I come to love
blue
      with the love of the childless

for the unborn?

RECOGNITION

Would the past know
me if it caught me?

>   Clumsy, jam-handed in overalls,
>   right eye shut, then left eye, fast

to make two truths at
once: *am*; *was*.

>   For years I believed
>   in my body, lying

down at night in rain,
waking into rain still falling

>   cold-alive inside that
>   name my brother calls me.

She was someone
I loved.

ANNIVERSARY

Do June again, for you have not gotten it quite.

What a passionless substance

this absence is, colors

summer in as if by number:

lemonade, trampledgrass, smalt — which is a deep & nearly
unforgivable blue. As it latens it dawdles, collects

all what's abandoned, the sunlight does.

An o'clock / an ochre filter.

The fossilized playground structures'

rusty spines. What extinct species of verb were once

mine? Run, jump, climb. Up the hot

metal bend of the slide. Shiny violence, this wistfulness — wants to put flesh on
the bones of it: feathers, scales, fingernails.

To see in the ginkgo tree's stinking seeds what

the world was. A substance, yet passionless. Not wanting anything but

to be truly without us,

for a branch tip to shoot out a leaf —

thus may each pollen cone release

its impeccable sporophylls, as it has always done — and go on

doing & doing that. June

was all strung up, like the ghostly diaphanous

slips on the fire escape at dusk — the undershirt barely

swaying like a rabbi praying

in his sleep, so sheer you saw the moon

sweat through, the dark all round — on our hopes for it.

A maculate

summer night far from the center, real far, almost close to the airport,

sprawl of vacant lots & used car dealerships is what we got.

An o'clock

like the other o'clocks. Except we had thought

I could walk. Pale prince in a kingdom of silverware I became

that night, that summer,

sat up

coloring the window: dark & dark & dark,

a deep substance, passionless. Swallowing

none of the vast sweep of feeling feasting on the joists of my

half-life, June just went on

polishing the horizon like a knife — a lost continent's edge,

Ability — agleam & neatly

placed back into the velvet drawer of night.

& maybe the trees, too — so black we

can't see them now — believed

they'd been promised a different arrangement,

not to kneel still as penitents until

the sky lucidly, scrupulously drops

its dioxides. We'd dreamed July

temperate: all ice cream & iridescence, even mosquitoes'

tinselflickering wings at our elbows expected, somehow correct. But the fact a plastic sac

of powdered-freezedried-then-diluted monoclonal antibodies stolen

from a mouse now drips

down into the roots of me —

that this substance, passionless, attacks

every cell

with its runoff of chemical snow —

put on a dress

feels like an outside joke. A laughter / a slaughter.

Like how I was somebody's daughter. How once we watched each other

with a terrible earnestness

& nothing anywhere breathing.

I was a mummy back then: someone

had painted a code on my body, a face on my face,

someone crushed spices into my absences, someone rinsed my insides with palm wine,

& I lay waiting

to disappear, or change.

You took the name

I gave you, and the thought you carry it

over the fields of your whole time

on earth cuts into me

like that post-IV ache in the vein, won't go away.

How to come back from that.

How to go out, like folks do, for a walk

— lemonade, trampledgrass — & not feel gone from it, not

take the whole gorgeous aftermath

personally? I try

to do June again, only this time we're not underwater —

down deep in the cold seeps, the abyssal

plain with its hagfish & boneworms & hundreds of atmospheres pressed on our hearts.

Remember?

How fear was our warmth down there, our shared

nourishment detritus of the secret

drifting relentlessly into our mouths, unspeakable.

Now it is out,

hung on these beached ribs, extinct & free,

I carry the ocean inside. In that vascular dark,

so much of my flesh was imaginary.

No one could see me. Only you could see me.

SAINT CONSEQUENCE

To trust a moon exists,
incandescent distance, is not to glimpse
a garden by the light of it.
Here now,
thrown against the wall, it makes a ghost
coin. The curtain's shadow casts a design
like a map you could cover the world in
if you could just line the edges up.
No
detail is refundable. No icon hauled up
from the past — *touch, unbeliever, the peeling-off*
face in its gold aureole, and remember —
can stare you back there.
I'd tell myself that
whenever wonder entered, then receded like the shy
drunk boy who didn't know anyone at the party
stumbling softly down the hallway, late.

I had to assume my experience mattered.
Knew if I could just peel back the clouds
there'd be a grid, or else a rip in the night's skin
leaking darkness,
but by the time I —
the surgeon performing
the autopsy — arrived, the corpse was
history. Now the scalpel is slippery; how
will I know where to make the cuts?

That boy leaned on a dumpster marked RECYCLABLES
and threw up. It seemed to take him a long time
and the muscles in his thin back tensed, released
with each new heave,
                  and my hand watched
his shoulder, untouching — lusting for the Y
chromosome nestled in each separate cell, and felt
love. Not for him so much
                        as for how an accretion
can make an argument if the grains cluster closely
enough, if the coastline bloats up
as the tide seeps out of it with a low, loud
sucking sound, then rears back to batter
an absence again.
                As if they've always been
attached that way, the parts.

He asked what god,
if any, I believed in, and the rain paused just like
listening — then went back to ripping, thread by
thread, the sky.
              Could I say why I
claw through dirt for that hard shine
like the other unbeloveds?
                One solid object
wrapped in the newspaper chaos of days to be
opened years later —
              as once under a streetlamp my grandmother
pulled the soaked scarf from her throat
full of sharp-edged German words, and sang —
feels like faith. It weighs, won't lighten.

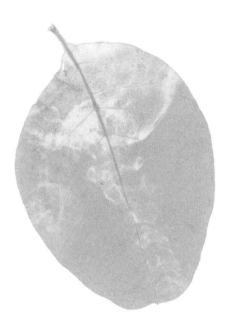

"The Civil Surgeon" borrows its title from the following passage on the official website of the U. S. Department of Homeland Security (http://www.uscis.gov): "Depending on the immigration benefit sought, an applicant may be required to undergo a medical examination. Immigration medical examinations conducted inside the United States must be performed by the civil surgeon who has been designated by USCIS (U.S. Citizenship and Immigration Services)."

My brother is the author of all of the words and phrases in the final section of "Brother."

The Russian epigraph to section two consists of the final lines of Aleksandr Vvedensky's poem "Gost' na kone:" "Ia zabyl / sushchestvovan'e, / ia sozertsal / vnov' / rasstoian'e."

The imagery in "Drone Pastoral" is based on Fazal Sheikh's *Desert Bloom* series, part of his four-volume *Erasure Trilogy* (Steidl, 2015).

In "Tomsk Mon Amour," the *Stalingrad Madonna* is a 1942 drawing by German soldier Kurt Reuber, sketched during the Battle of Stalingrad. Copies of the original, which hangs in the Kaiser Wilhelm Memorial Church in Berlin, can be found in other cathedrals in Berlin, Coventry, and Volgograd, as a symbol of post-WWII reconciliation between Russia and Western Europe.

"Street of the Friendship of Nations" grew out of my time in and around the Siberian city of Tomsk, where I lived from 2010 to 2011, and to which I returned in 2015. Much of the imagery is drawn from photographs, both my own and those I encountered through research on the early Soviet era. "Krokodil" is the slang name for desomorphine, a synthetic opioid. A "dacha" is a small second home with a garden, located in the exurbs of post-Soviet cities and formerly allotted to citizens by the state for the purpose of growing their own food. The word "dacha" comes from the Russian "davat'," "to give."

The word "crip" in "Crip Album," formerly a slur against those with mobility impairments, has been reclaimed as an identification by many people in the disability community, including myself.

"The Center" speaks to my experiences of moving through the so-called "second world" as a white, Western subject in the early twenty-first century. I have resisted specifying a singular location for the poem—both in order to focus on the feeling and situation of tourism, and to avoid the appearance of trying to "capture" any of the places described. The italicized words come from section XV of Wallace Stevens's "Ésthetique du Mal:" "The greatest poverty is not to live / In a physical world, to feel that one's desire / Is too difficult to tell from despair."

"Blue Screen Pastoral" is indebted to Osip Mandelstam's image of "mineral rock as a diary of the weather" in his essay "Conversation About Dante" [«Разговор о Данте»] (ca. 1934).

ACKNOWLEDGMENTS

Thank you to the following journals, in which several of these poems first appeared, often in earlier versions:

32 Poems: "Blue Screen Pastoral"

The Adroit Journal: "Cut," "The Civil Surgeon," "Vantage Point"

Bellevue Literary Review: "Drought Pastoral"

Best New Poets 2020: "Anniversary"

Columbia Journal: "Gender Clinic"

Conjunctions: "Cut," "The Civil Surgeon"

Deerfield Public Library Queer Poem-a-Day: "An Act"

LARB Quarterly Journal: "Tarkovsky"

The Kenyon Review: "Near-Disappearance," "Trans People of the Past"

The Offing: "On Devotion"

Narrative: "Saint Consequence"

Poets.org: "Anniversary"

This book could not have come into being without the support of the Northwestern University Creative Writing Program, the University of Michigan's Helen Zell Writers' Program, Harvard University's Graduate School of Arts and Sciences, and Earlham College— and the many teachers, colleagues, students, and friends who make these places what they are. Special thanks to my mentors: Mary Kinzie, Clare Cavanagh, Reginald Gibbons, Averill Curdy, Stephanie Burt, Stephanie Sandler, Jorie Graham, Peter Sacks, Sumita Chakraborty, Katie Peterson, and Linda Gregerson.

A poet is nothing without a community. I am deeply grateful to those generous readers and dear friends who have strengthened my thinking and writing over the years: Calista McRae, Elizabeth Metzger, Ashley Keyser, rl Goldberg, David Freeman, Zahir Janmohamed, Claire Robison, Ainsley Morse, Lusia Zaitseva, Ted Hixson, Marta Figlerowicz, Elizabeth

Weckhurst, and the members of Zoomshop. And to Maia Kelner, who gets me.

Many thanks to Carey Salerno, Alyssa Neptune, Emily Marquis, Lacey Dunham, Genevieve Hartman, and the Alice James Books family. I couldn't be happier to make a home in your pages. Thank you also to Megan Bent for your art.

Finally, endless gratitude to my parents, for listening. To Matthew, the silence behind all of these words, I love you. *Kooma shooma.*

And to Madeline—this one's for you.

RECENT TITLES FROM ALICE JAMES BOOKS

Alice James Books is committed to publishing books that matter. The press was founded in 1973 in Boston, Massachusetts to give women access to publishing. As a cooperative, authors performed the day-to-day undertakings of the press. The press continues to expand and grow from its formative roots, guided by its founding values of access, excellence, inclusivity, and collaboration in publishing. Its mission is to publish books that matter and preserve a place of belonging for poets who inspire us. AJB seeks to broaden our collective interpretation of what constitutes the American poetic voice and is dedicated to helping its artists achieve purposeful engagement with broad audiences and communities nationwide. The press was named for Alice James, sister to William and Henry, whose extraordinary gift for writing went unrecognized during her lifetime.

Designed by Zoe Norvell

Printed by Versa Press